We find the amazing in the ordinary every day with lists, polls and quizzes. Helping us to appreciate, in fun and quirky ways, the world in which we live.

Creating interactive content, R Amazing! is a safe place to explore different topics and share your views.

It is ok to disagree with us regarding who or what we think is amazing! We share our thoughts on our website and in our books to enable debate and discussion.

We encourage the expression of opinions in an appropriate way with an understanding that it is ok for people to have differing views.

R Amazing! debates should be conducted politely and respectfully, ending with an agreement and common ground, even if that is to agree to disagree.

www.r-amazing.com

Mythical Creatures R Amazing
Markus Baker & Adam Galvin

Published by R-and-Q.com.

ISBN: 978-1-9161450-5-4

MYTHICAL CREATURES R AMAZING!

Adam Galvin and Markus Baker
Creators of 'People R Amazing!'

"*Everything you can imagine is real.*"

Pablo Picasso

*Logic will get you
from A to Z;...*

...imagination will get you everywhere.

Albert Einstein

LEARN MORE AT
www.r-amazing.com/yeti/

The Yeti

Whilst looking for an alternative route to climb Mt. Everest, British Explorer – Eric Shipton, stumbled upon a footprint of the amazing Yeti. He took a picture of the creature's footprint for all to see. Yeti originated from a Sherpa word meaning "Wildman" another title given to this amazing legend is "Abominable Snowman".

The Yeti has been described as having a muscular body like an ape, with white shaggy fur that is taller than the average human. Scientists claim there is not enough hard evidence to prove its existence. However, for enthusiasts, photo evidence and sightings may prove otherwise. What do you think?

> *There is precious little in civilization to appeal to a yeti.*
> Edmund Hillary

> *During the 1950s, almost
> every Western explorer who
> ventured into the Himalayas
> brought back tales of the Yeti.*
>
> Prof. Geller

*Whatever is the truth,
there is no denying that
Nessie will continue to
intrigue the world
for years to come.*
Jonathan Bright

LEARN MORE AT
www.r-amazing.com/loch-ness/

The Loch Ness Monster

According to legend, the Loch Ness Monster, lovingly known as Nessie, was first reported in 1933 inhabiting the deep, cold waters of the Loch Ness in Scotland. Since then, many locals and tourists have claimed to have seen the great beast and many debate the origins of the Loch Ness monster, some believing that it dates to the dinosaur age and is a large reptile. Currently, there is no hard evidence that proves the existence of this mythical creature. On the other hand, reports, photos and scientific investigations suggest differently. Whether you believe it or not – there's no smoke without fire! You decide.

> *If Nessie is 70 to 80 feet long, swims as fast as a motorboat and looks like a long-necked dinosaur, then we saw her.*
> Patricia Diaz, 1996

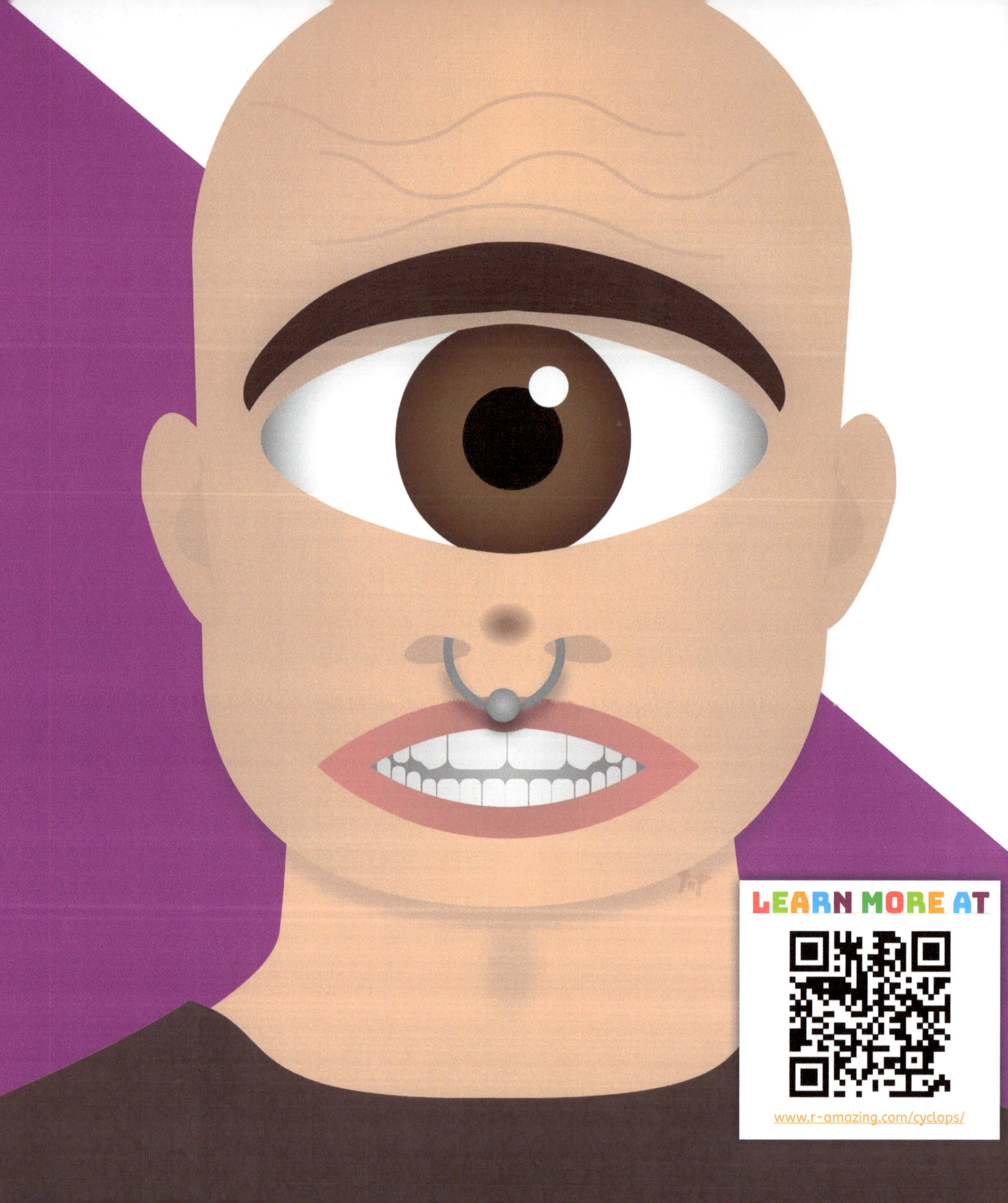
LEARN MORE AT
www.r-amazing.com/cyclops/

Cyclops

The word cyclops literally means "round-eyed" or "circle-eyed" and originates from Greek Mythology and had a foul disposition and feasted upon humans. They were thought to have been locked away in the fiery depths of the Underworld, however, they were later released from their hellish prison by the Greek Gods.

Many scholars believe the legend of the cyclops came from blacksmiths, who wore an eyepatch covering one eye to prevent them from becoming blind in both eyes from flying sparks. They were also reported to have tattooed circles in honour of the sun.

Do cyclops exist? A baby goat with one enlarged eye has been born in Assam, India. The kid was born and baffled local villagers. The condition has been reported in other animals, such as horses, pigs, cows, cats and even dusky sharks.

Cyclopes are massive, lumbering beasts, so tall that a grown man would still fall below their knees.

Prof. Geller

Described as half woman and half fish, with long hair, a finely shaped nose and large eyes many sailors were lured and 'experienced the first effects of love' as they gazed upon them before their peril.

LEARN MORE AT
www.r-amazing.com/mermaids/

Mermaid

The first stories of mermaids appeared in ancient times and were associated with perilous events, misfortune and death, luring sailors off course into grave danger. Described as half woman and half fish, with long hair, a finely shaped nose and large eyes many sailors were lured and 'experienced the first effects of love' as they gazed upon them before their peril.

There have been accounts of mermaids reported by the famous explorer Christopher Columbus during one of his explorations to the Caribbean. There have also more recently been many sightings of Mermaids, but no hard evidence exists to date. In 2009 a town in Israel offered a one million reward to the first person that photographed the creature. No photographs surfaced. Was it a hoax or, did the mermaid sense its demise? Do mermaids really exist? That's for you to decide, just be careful when travelling on a boat!

LEARN MORE AT
www.r-amazing.com/medusa/

Medusa

Legend has it anyone who looked directly at Medusa would instantly turn to stone. She is said to have the features of a hideous woman with venomous snakes upon her head instead of hair. Known as a Gorgon, Medusa was a Greek monster, who was punished for falling in love with Poseidon. Eventually, Medusa was killed when Perseus cut her head off. Even though Medusa is a Greek Myth have you ever met someone who stares into your soul? Who makes you feel stone-cold and freeze on the spot? Maybe Medusas are among us hidden in plain sight. You decide.

> *The television, that insidious beast, like Medusa freezes a billion people to stone every night, staring fixedly, that Siren which called and sang and promised so much and gave, after all, so little.*
> Ray Bradbury

Even though Medusa is a Greek Myth have you ever met someone who stares into your soul? Who makes you feel stone-cold and freeze on the spot?

Ancient cultures wrote of the Unicorn as a real animal. In fact, it was included in many natural history books of the time.
Prof. Geller

LEARN MORE AT
www.r-amazing.com/unicorns/

Unicorn

Unicorns are mythical and date all the way back to ancient carvings. Interestingly, these seem to be the only mythical creature that is not based upon human fears. Described as having a white body, purple head, blue eyes, and a multicoloured horn (red at the top, black in the middle, and white at the base). They are strong, pure animals, who are solitary.

Are unicorns still among us? Just because humans cannot see the horn does it mean they are not there? Is it hidden in plain sight, beyond our depth of sight perception?

> *Among other things, the unicorn was thought to hold the cure to many sicknesses, the ability to purify water, and the antidote to poisons in its horn.*
>
> Prof. Geller

LEARN MORE AT
www.r-amazing.com/pope-lick/

The Pope Lick

Some tales say that the Pope Lick is a mythical circus freak born within the circus community. Legend has it he wanders looking for his next victim wielding an axe and using a hypnotic voice to coerce them to their doom.

Crossed between a human and a goat, the Pope Lick has a muscular deformed body. It is partly covered in fur with wide-set eyes and sharp protruding horns jutting out of thick hair.

Does the Pope Lick exist? You may well find out the next time a travelling fair visit.

> *The Pope Lick uses it's hypnotic voice to coerce people to their doom.*

*Crossed between a human
and a goat, the Pope Lick has
a muscular deformed body.*

*A man on a horse is spiritually,
as well as physically,
bigger than a man on foot.*

John Steinbeck

LEARN MORE AT
www.r-amazing.com/centaurs/

Centaur

A Centaur with the body and hind legs of a horse attached to the upper half of a human torso.

Most Centaurs were known as obnoxious, vulgar and loud, with one exception - Chiron, who was known for his skills and intelligence.

In Greek Mythology Chiron trained heroes such as Achilles and Jason.

Although Centaurs are Mythology they may very well be among us. Have you ever seen a horse in perfect harmony with its rider?

> *Technically, we're all half centaur.*
> Nick Offerman

LEARN MORE AT
www.r-amazing.com/cupid/

Cupid

Holding a small bow with a quiver filled with golden arrows, Cupid, is the Roman god of beauty and love. Historically, he is often depicted as having a baby-like appearance, chubby body, baby face and soft feathered wings.

He is known for firing golden arrows at people to make them fall in love and heavy arrows to make others fall out of love. This is his source of power! Have you ever been struck by the invisible arrow of Cupid's bow?

> *Love is the answer.*
> *The question is unimportant.*
> Jeff Foster

*Love cannot live
where there is no trust.*

Edith Hamilton

*To look into the eyes
of a wolf is to see
your own soul.*

Aldo Leopold

LEARN MORE AT
www.r-amazing.com/werewolf/

Werewolf

The haunting howl, a full moon and the sight of a wolf-like creature with thick fur, snarling jaws of terror and a powerful torso can only mean one thing. The werewolf is a mythical creature that derives from 'wer' meaning man and 'wulf' meaning wolf. Legend has it that a werewolf can only be killed with a silver bullet.

Do we all turn into werewolves? According to some research and experts, it's possible the moon can affect our behaviour. Even though we cannot see any physical changes, our mood changes. Next time the moon is full take notice of your mood!

> *I think we all have to fight the werewolf within us somehow.*
> William Kempe

My picture of the most amazing mythical creature.

The most amazing mythical creature is

....

I love it when this amazing mythical creature...

....

....

....

....

....

....

This mythical creature is amazing because...

....

....

....

....

*"Mythical creatures
don't really exist."*

The reply…

... "That depends on whether or not there's someone who can see them."

Jodi Picoult

MORE BOOKS BY R&Q

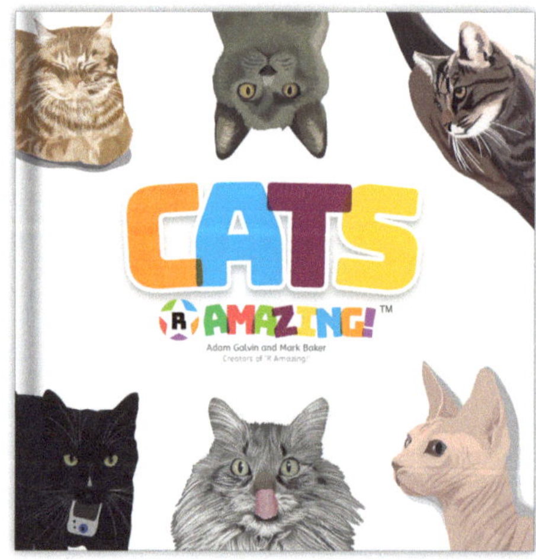

check out the books and merchandise at

www.R-and-Q.com